NIGHTSEASONS

By Peter Cooley

The Company of Strangers (1975)
The Room Where Summer Ends (1979)
Nightseasons (1983)

Peter Cooley

NIGHTSEASONS

Carnegie-Mellon University Press
Pittsburgh 1983
Feffer and Simons, Inc., London

Acknowledgments

Acknowledgment is gratefully made to the editors of the following magazines in which most of these poems first appeared:

"The Other," *The New Yorker* "For Alissa," (as "The Night Season"), *Mississippi Review*; "Autumn Equinox," "Psalm: The Roaring," *Prairie Schooner*; "No One," "To the Statue of a Young Satyr," "Nightpiece," "After Men, After Women," *Poetry Now*; "Small Prayer," "How Many," *Ponchrtrain Review*; "Nightfall," *Southern Review*; "In the Crepuscular," *Racoon*; "Psalm," ("I would draw near this child, God"), *The Memphis State Review*; "Psalm," ("Let the sea come to me when I am old"), *Amicus*; "The Secret," *The New Jersey Poetry Journal*; "It Witness," "Certain Stars," "He," *The Kansas Quarterly*; "The Last Gift," *The Sonora Review*; "The Last Testament of Pierre Duval," (as "Desire"), *Porch*; "Toward Morning," "To a Child, A Spring Poem," *The Barat Review*; "To a Wasp Caught in the Storm Sash at the Advent of the Winter Solstice," *Southern Poetry Review*; "The Unasked For," *The Georgia Review*; "The Egaltine," *The Devil's Millhopper*; "The Carp Pond," "Ode to the Statutes," *Northeast*; "Chrysanthemum Light," *Akros*; "Frog Hunting," *The Yale Review*; "The Sparrows," *Crazy Horse*; "To the Stillborn," *The Missouri Review*; "Assumptions," *Negative Capability*; "The Mutability Poem," "Lines for a Sleeping Child," "The Cicadas," "Crows Over the Wheatfield," "The Gull," *Midwest Poetry Review*; "The Night Speaks to a Man," "Necessities," "Such Comfort as the Night Can Bring," "The Lilies," *The Sewanee Review*; "The Elect," *Ohio Review*; "The Other" appeared in *Anthology of Magazine Verse and Yearbook of American Poetry 1980*.

The publication of this book is supported by grants from the National Endowment for the Arts, a Federal agency, and from the Pennsylvania Council on the Arts.

The author wishes to thank Ossabaw Island, where some of these poems were written, and the Division of the Arts of the State of Louisiana for a creative writing fellowship which allowed for the writing of poems and the preparation of this manuscript. To Alice Voros and Rosemary Eddins particular thanks are due for their assistance.

Library of Congress Catalog Card Number 82-074302
ISBN 0-915604-82-5
ISBN 0-915604-83-3 Pbk.

Printed and bound in the United States of America
First Edition

CONTENTS

For Nicole and Alissa

the night shineth as the day; the darkness and
the light are both alike to thee.

--Psalm 139

But is there any comfort to be found?
Man is in love and loves what vanishes,
What more is there to say?

--Yeats,
Nineteen Hundred and Nineteen

NIGHTTHOUGHTS

NO ONE

Across the autumns, the cold fields bared
for winter and the whole night sky
one prism in the lake's first ice,
I hear my father calling me.
It is my mother he is drawing to him.
And that accomplished, every elm,
its last leaves in the green moonlight
laden with frost, and the pine, resinous,
the milkweed, the cattail, each bows down
to bear this wind again.
They right themselves, approach me, each a gift.

Which shadow, soul, is yours?
Which stalk or tendril calls you home
these nights I am unborn
in mid-November? When I am motherless,
fatherless, and, standing in the wind,
such shadow as becomes the wind,
bole, branch, stem and vein
each my held breath
perilous with anticipation.

THE UNASKED FOR

There, at the other side,
where afternoon steps down,
fluted between the willows,
and draws its shape from them
till stem, bole, root
become the night, invisible,
the Mississippi is another river.

Here, it is this minute.
Or this one, scummed, lapping, empurpled.
From the highroad of the levee
I stare out over the depths,
a small daughter at each hand.
Sundays are glass jars
on our side, sapphire, emerald
fluttering wings inside them.
They are bouquets of open air.

The barges' pearl wake, the bargemen
muttering their arcane tongue,
the sky over my shadow, violet,
and the noon, scintillant, breaking across it--
I have brought them up here
that they remember years from now
nothing of this, nothing but this:
when the light staggers on our side
and on that other, across the water
unasked for, darkness starts.
And then, trembling, the willows
follow, to bear us down
with their wind, headfirst, staggering.
And take such night to us
that only the fingers inside mine
assure me we are here together,
a day they may remember if at all
a lightning bug, a father shadowless, this starless water.

NOCTURNE

First night terror of a small daughter:
already it is in her blood
by the time you scoop her up,
kiss the neckcurls, the white heat
ablaze in her tears and chatter.

She stammers, *witch, moon, bat,*
pointing to the dark glass
the night swims in, her lifeline
racing to it, stumbling on sounds,
star, monster, her voice warbling
to take wing.
         She takes, soaring.

You walk with her. You ride the air,
knowing how soon she must come down.
How the night will sing if she lifts to it
such tiny music as might fix the dark
to lighten it: silence and dread,
all images' beginning.

ON THE FIRST MORNING OF MY THIRTY- NINTH YEAR

The sea returns, unasked for,
to the sea wall, the sky comes back
mornings demanding nothing,
stunning us with light.
After the long midnight
this curtain of banyan trees at dawn
lifts an instant on the terrace,
the curtain of dove song rises,
curtain of gnat and sea rose
incarnadine, curtain of pelican, gull . . .

If this is my soul
it is a tiny thing here taking wing
at the end of my body
among the invisibles, singing to me . . .

Who would have believed the world
would be so long in coming
half my words have burned away?
Who could have invented this presence
reflecting the surface of morning,
restoring weight to the stones,
the roots to trees the day takes on
imperfect, wholly mortal, vanishing.

CERTAIN STARS

How tiny a thing she is, my daughter.
Under her fingers a world crooks
wolf-jawed or serpentine, one she calls up
later tonight, terrifying herself
chiaroscuro on the wall.

How on our walk this afternoon
she climbs and then slips back,
redescends and forks the waterfall
of her own speech. How, scattering the air,
she breaks herself and cannot cease
until words take her between sleep and waking.

How at her step the earth gives way,
and to mine now, bending for her hand.
In this last light continents divide
along our street; rivers surrender banks
vermillion where the sidewalk ends.

How before us the cold light, gold,
the light, falling against us, vanishes.
And in her stare, the sky, wide-eyed,
returns my own and these stars, dark,
I brought her to tonight
before I had taught myself to name them.

TO MY DAUGHTER

Because you would not let me go.
Because I could not let you go.
Because the room stood over us
still dancing and the blue light reeled
at the window and we staggered
until I tore myself from you,
your tiny hands grappling at the air . . .

This is the reason for the poem.

And this: when I became no father
at the morning's other side
but a man, anyone, barreling to work,
I turned back and at the window caught your face:
here, behind the caul of glass,
topaz in your eyes
I'd never found reflection in,
I saw my own the years had finished
half-lidded, stillborn in expectation.

PSALM

I would draw near this child, God,
my daughter, a stranger to me.
She whom her mother ripped from death
nine years has kept the world
a firmament in her eyes
while my own weigh heavy with onyx.

Yet still trusts she the wasp on our peony,
the rose and the rose thorn, the ivy,
the man chortling, calling her close
to the fence, who opens his pants.

Even as the oak, God, in our yard
shot past me from my watering,
or my friend took my advice,
cast off his loss and ceased to write,
she will ring by ring outstrip me.
To her littleness, then, will I sing this
while the olive tree plays to the wind in it.
Not till the end of time
but the little that she can give me.

FROG HUNTING

Almost always ahead of us,
hippety, in the night,
their sixth sense
radar to pick us up
and give them, hippety,
one jump on us,
the frogs dot the sidewalk
of summer after rain.
They are pursued, hop,
by two little girls,
barefoot, hair loose
in their faces, their hands
hippety, clasped in mine,
tugging this tired father.
Through sidestreets, the puddles
like black marshes, the concrete
buckled and split, hip-
pety, I'm pulled, hop.
But should a tired frog,
hippety, a lazy one,
a dreamer, one fat
with too many flies
or a frogleg-watching stud,
hippety, happen to pause
and feet of a demoiselle or two
land on his clamminess,
then, hippety, hippety, up
the father's legs they jump
to be carried, shrieking,
one in each arm, wriggling,
home to their mother, hop.

TWO FOR A SMALL DAUGHTER

I

NIGHT THOUGHTS

At last you are asleep.
The father in you, the mother in you,
exiled in the south--
and warring in your small limbs
which would take down the sky
to the bayou, to the mudflats--
have collapsed with your dolls on the bed.

Now the night can come
flooding out of your body
to meet that other in the garden
waiting for you since birth.
Little neckcurls, at my touch
swansoft, snow-downed cheeks
I bend to kiss, you enclose nothing!
Neither of us is here
to catch at tusks, the lifted hoof
your mobile throws on the wall.

Already with me! We stalk the wind,
calling him Great Father, Great-Grandfather,
scattering our word where the Queen Palm,
Confederate Jasmine, the Live Oak
bow before us, shadowless
on the black grass . . . and each cold leaf
rings bells of frost that we should walk
together beyond body, you and I.

II

ROWING SONG

Little one, like us the stars nod off
after midnight. They stretch out and stretch out,
drifting slowly into that cold vault
strewn this evening with their stare,
each tiny eye fixed in a wink.
Row! Row! Row! Or pass the oars
so I can pull us home
through the clear mirror of the green lagoon
the nightsky will collapse in after dark.
But these stars . . . since you are young
you might dare to wish on one
while I have made out in their reflection
the chillest sleep I've ever dreamed of
and then, beneath it, fractured by the lilies,
your face and mine, those long, cold stretches
where constellations never see themselves
nor ever reach to touch. Nor speak.
And there it is that we begin.

FOR ALISSA

This is a poem for my daughter,
her of the topaz eye reflecting mine
eight years into the world.
Women have told me my eyes are like a statue's,
unmoving, cold. Hers never stop dancing.

Nor does her little body
lost to a plié or the dark woods
in the midst of Brothers Grimm
surrender its sharp grip
on the ground under it, spinning.
Nor on the wind over her always lifting.

Who from her mother was ripped
before her time and clung to Death
three days until he fell.
Who cocks her head like a bear cub
at my approach, moving too fast
that I should touch her with my expectation.

Who in a night season
seven years back
when I lay in terror of myself
cried out and drew me to her
hours while I walked her.
That tiny head pressed to my shoulder
downed with hair fine as cowslip
or the soft, white fire of milkweed
spilling over my skin--
and lifted these wings here
nubby, oracular, stubborn,
which brought me to morning,
nudging their small way upward.

ASSUMPTIONS

THE SECRET

Because I was too much with myself
and myself, I went down to the sea this evening.
The tide was in, and all along the sand
the dead were waiting: auger and whelk,
pecten and conch, cast up, cast back again,
rattling their spines, the green waves diced with foam.
The sea looked straight at me--
it wouldn't flinch, this funny cemetery
while I stretched out among the tombs
surrendering the black light in my limbs,
my head, to drown it.

And now, sitting here tonight
I hear the dead at my desk
talking to the dead, lamenting.
The sea stalls in my arms and legs,
knocks at my eyes, asking for a word, any word.

I had no one to tell this to but you.

NIGHTFALL

Let these bathers go home
to bury their legs, their arms, their faces
in each other or television--

this gulf wind graze my bare skin
between the shoulders and, thinning, colder,
tilt the chalice of its voice to my lips--

let the skyline call for the last rites,
the sun set about reincarnation
along the Ganges, the Bering Strait--

the sandcrabs crawl out to hunt
like ghosts blown over this beach
the rat stalks, lying with rats

the moon will bless, let star
discover star or dragonfly and lizard
lizard, frogs in chorus warbling.

Little god pelican, little god gull,
I have watched all day for an instant
when I can find nothing but night:

this must be how I want to wait, standing
knee-deep, waist-deep in breakers,
up to my neck in salt spray, praying to no one.

THE LAST GIFT

Tonight my mother, dinner over
alone or with the widows
she names friends,
walks the shingle of gulf water,
the twilight violet on her rings.
Far from my father,
the old house in the North,
she is barefoot, halfway through her seventies,
and the water is emerald and then clear
this mid-December as she stoops
to claim a shark tooth, a sand dollar.

The voice which walked above me
by the cold waters of Lake Huron
resinous with pine and parted them
to take me in, who named the stars,
the roaring at the Royal Oak Zoo,
the first seedling in the garden
streaked with frost and sang the night asleep,
rests now within her finally.
What last word did it bend to give me
in the garden by the fishpond?
Was it forsythia which at that moment fell?
What name did she give me for the rock?
What kind of luminescence did she spell into my hand?

PSALM

Let the sea come to me when I am old
as I come to it tonight. Furying,
let the breakers climb the black rocks
winnowing their emerald. Let the spindrift
rack the shingle and the date palm
make obeisance to the swell of wind.
Now, mid-life, I go to the birds,
tracking wood ibis, loon, spoonbill,
even grateful for this small tern at my side
whose feathers catch the last light
as I can't, ivory ruffling--
later the birds will come to me
and the thunderheads, basso profundo,
the lightning, the stars which will rain down.
Let the sea come to me that night
when its last word will be the silence
the sea maintained this noon
turning its perfect face upright,
concealing nothing, featureless,
shadowless beyond recognition.

HOW MANY

I will die. The seagulls cry that to me,
drifting above the breakers, calling
each other, calling. In three days it is Spring.

I will lie down on an ordinary night,
not one like this: the gulf wind fire
at sunset, the waves walking it,
flame passing into flame.

I will be high tide and low tide
the same instant, when the world
stands over my bed, a huge breath
pressed to mine. My eyes will flood with dark.
All at once I will throw it from me.

But these gulls-- how warm the eggs are
speckling the sand, later. How many cries
the white breast lifts over the water
only to touch some other a few hours
and pass on, calling to another.

SMALL PRAYER

Tag end of afternoon.

The ocean deepens to cinnabar.
In the pines night settles,
darkness stiffening the needles,
floats the host, the white pine scent,
to die, sweet, on the water.
Votive, scarlet and violet
the primroses shake their wicks.

I am freight on my own hands,
my blossoms rust, they stand up
on the last attempt, next to last. . .

But you, transparent as snail's wake,
glister cresting the sponges,
little spirit I call from the breakers,
walk with me after dinner here.
Diminish me as the night falls,
let me be waves, their headstones
high tides under our feet.
Let me grow smaller, seagull's shadow,
cast me down, tinier, tinier,
dragonfly, wasp on a dark cusp,
wings on water, absence of wings.

A CORONAL

When the sky closes down
the gulls take back their shadows
from the high tide, from the white grains
the sand crab resumes its own
and stepping out, the wild horses theirs
when the grasses are thrown open to release them.

The sea burns off the sea rose
at the last reaches of its leaves
and darkness floods the heart,
the petals, which are one again.

He is a small thing being a man
under the azure shadow of heaven
taken back into himself.
Here, at the end of the last light
he hears a fury of small wings
descending, as if under his breath.
Seize on him, demons, and possess him.

ASSUMPTIONS

Everything is more than possible again:
the sea, refusing to lie still,
continues ritual ministrations
of the shore, it is possible.
And the sky, floating isles of palms,
a gold dome limitless at dawn.

Stepping out of the house,
I step down, kneeling in myself,
striated by shadows of gulls
to see my body as another
the beach has waited for
eternally lifting its white hands.

What vows at world's beginning
these heavens pledged the earth
to keep its edge in spasms,
high tide, low. What oaths
eons ago their ancestors
extracted from the wind
that these gulls arrange themselves,
assume another morning at their feet.
That they should call me
as if one of their kind
to walk the breakers.
That I assume I will pretend I can.

HE

Which of you, if I should name him,
in the night season when I speak at last,
will deny me this, my soul?
Who insist he is a shadow
walking beside me with the sea
this evening, falling everywhere at once
and the hightide, waist-high, emerald, breaking.

Which friend will take from me
the darkness I ascend to
while he speaks, describe him
as but another gull
the gulf wind turns and freezes
here at the still-point on the wind
to which the sea grapes gather
with the sea oats, lying down--
who cast off the locust's long note
he has lifted to surrender?

Those who believe in their lives
stretching before them, limitless
as this ocean, luminous
where the sky falls, vanishing
can leave us here:

And now he has left me
wordless, to go forth with him
tomorrow, naming the afterlight,
the day after that--

knowing the nights I crossed to get here
and after how many years
what a small thing I am still
waiting to assume him, finally.

THE ROARING

THE ELECT

Many the shadowless under the rose leaves
untrembling midmorning.
Many at early evening
the wings, ochre, henna, cinnabar,
which continue, unseen, singing
when night, never stirring, takes their air.

In this garden out of time
the stillborn until their moment linger.
Their souls climb the white down
of little tubers, footless; they suck
mouthless the orris root. Hoarfrost
their spoor foreshadows them, burned off by noon.

And from this place we called the child to us
that you might carry it
to give it up. And spare her breath
this life, the agony of body, the next, the next, the next.
Tonight on the long, clear wing of her voice
the soul of our daughter walks out
between the thorns, uplifted, no one

warbling her absence, everlasting.

THE SPARROWS

By the time it comes to me
I will have ceased speaking
even to myself, the woman thinks.
On the window evening deepens
beyond her yard, and at the river
the willows, in the shallows waist-high,
already lie down with the first dark.

Her cold palms lift her breasts.
Lighter, they slip from her.
At her belly the fingers web
over this child, unmoving now
she will surrender tomorrow, still.

Yet how this first appeared,
the river gone over to the dark,
the acanthus and jasmine little flames
the pane divided up, she cannot put away.
How the frost parted and the grass
flickered, then stood still
that first instant, quickening,
And after that, how the light fell
on the sparrows she had not seen before.
How, without echo, their screams arose
before them, and the shrub gave up
blossom to seed that they might sing,
each bearing upward before it
the token moment of its survival.

TO THE STILLBORN

Too soon now this grief will have passed from me.
I will wake up tomorrow, the day after,
and my roaring will be the hills
laying themselves down in gold
on the evening, empurpled, no longer.

No longer the dogwood my moan
at first light, nor the redbud
my weeping, not branch by branch
as they draw the sky down to their falling.

On a morning ordinary
as steam rising from my coffee
trawling the night after it
and the nights before, gnashing and tossing,
you will abandon me suddenly--
this anguish, was it too great
enthroning me, crowning me, sceptre in hand,
for you to-- bow down?

Today I take my pain again
into my own hands here, unroll it--
a scroll? The script is too tiny.
I like not being able to read it.
Now I put it on, strut about
wearing my hair shirt. How I love the hurt!

When you reach wherever you're going that morning
you will have shaken me off, immortal.
Little one, no name,
you will no longer be my daughter.

PSALM: THE ROARING

I

Unless the sky take me in when I roar to it
my loss will not weigh less upon me.

Unless the ground open beneath me
that I know a dwelling place
in bedrock, or, cast in marl,
splay my bones, fan-tailed,
that they cease to lead me but follow.

It is vain to tell others or keep to oneself
the loss of a child not a child.
I turn on myself, on this word
too sculpted, which should describe
the tracery of a leaf, rare swans, an ivory sword,
the color of Irish tea: *stillborn.*

II

"Daughters are a gift from the Lord"
but this was no daughter, no one
but gobbets of skin and blood
like the pieces of someone I had loved
after an aircrash.

As much shibboleth to us who loved her
while she trained inside her mother,
a dancer keeping the sky
under each kick, her plies, her entrechats,
orbiting to release it--

as the earth in the garden I upturned
next to the garage last week:
those baby rats like meat spit up
undigested, stringy and red.
They must have been dead just an hour.

Irretrievable, it must be put from us
to begin to suffer grief.

THE EGLANTINE

Nevertheless, the sky goes on righting itself.
Nevertheless, lust shows up,
insists, does what lust knows best,
shrinks away. Nevertheless, the maw calls,
jackdaw hooked to its perch in the wall
to be stuffed to satiety.

I walk to the faucet to get a drink.
At the window I stand, my back to you.
I choose the blue cut glass
and when I've drained it, lift the absence
so the afternoon pours down
torrents glistening emerald.

Later there will be rain or not
and that will be dropped, picked up,
as our tongues slide over this distance
until the demands of evening
crawl, speckled, horn-ornamented,
out of the shadows,
toenails scratching the tiles.

What does it trouble the sky
that we go on grieving

the child we buried this morning?
The sky goes on falling,
thunderheads gather, disperse,
the ground goes on righting itself.
While beyond us, where the town ends,
the lawns stretch out and then the river,
violet, turns until empurpled
willows lie down along the banks.
And beside them the hawthorne, the little yews,
the myrtle, ivies stiffen in the chill
like the profusion of the eglantine
already soaked with night
or the cut flowers strewn at ten a.m.
darkening the heaped up earth
giving way already at either hand
to the tiny alabaster level with the ground.

THE INHABITANT

So, you are back.
Your little legs turkey trot
the morning beach, shadowless.
You waddle down to it
as if, because bodiless
like you, the sea were yours.

Little ghost,
little seed of me buried
in a distant city,
I want the seascape others seek.
I dropped the words I dug up
back in the earth, my names for you.
I confessed my sin in dredging
for poetry in your loss.
And yet you will not let me go.
Among beachwalkers arm in arm,
the blare of rock-and-roll,
the boy dragging his girl down
into the tides, you turn toward me
the featureless white linen of your face.

TO A CHILD, A SPRING POEM

Along the boulevards the first camellias
lift their lush fire like flambeaux to the twilight
erect, processional. In the live oak
the mockingbird takes up her shriek again,
and by the black lagoon the dragonfly
assumes, above the timpani of crickets,
its iridescent, slow descent over the lilies.
This is the hour the fathers are coming home.
They are crossing the yards, the cold, sallow ground,
bearing the children in their arms
as I take you, up to the darkening houses.
And, had you lived, we would be inside now,
snug, out of sight. We would not stand together
holding up this sky night after night,
our backs against the wind--
my words wind and yours not even that
and the stars, the dark stars, an instant, vanishing.

REFUSING TO DIMINISH

THE LILIES

Today I can hear autumn in my voice.
The first clear strain like ice
quickens at the pond's center,
where the dead stars, which will engulf me later,
scud up as cusps of lilies, stiffening.
Why cry the advent of another season?
When I cast darkness from my spring
I had only to lie down, their trumpets at my side
and blossoms spoke through me, which I allowed
like my eye floating the stems summer at noon
too late.
      Too late but for this word
I taught myself about a vein along a pod,
the staggering blooms, all flowering,
the root I haven't come to yet,
the long diminishings.

ODE TO THE STATUES

I

There can be no proper dark.
There is but this one, walking with me
and whatever I can seize of you
between your bodies, beyond fury here
in the garden. And the earth
flowering from its nether root
you refuse to assume.
Do with me what you will.

II

Bronze does not hold you
nor marble which you burst
conceived. Nor does the wind
over which you play a music
I can never hear
but in instants surrendering
the body I bring here.
Let me set it down beside yours on the air.

III

This is what it is to die:
your breath under mine, your stiffness
at my extremities, to climb the azure,
these lineaments of pure desire,
hoping to trace you and fall back--
that I should go on suffering such dark
as I arrange about you, knowing it myself.

THE CICADAS

I

When the world leaves me
it will be like this:
one cry answering mine
from the catalpa, the air black flame
taking me in, rising.
One voice a single scream
swarming under my breath.

II

Awakening, the dead rise,
shake themselves out
of the last life, assume the air,
invisible, the upper branches.
How clear the music is,
the soul sings, arriving,
how clear, beyond sound.

III

While the breath leaves him
his voice is torn off
and in terror the man waits
his final seconds, no one.

And then the scream
beyond him, in his voice--
he feels his soul stretch out
bodiless along that song.

IV

Tonight under the cry
I stand, rooted in silence
the tree one word, unspeakable.

And the tree stills, hearing this,
the darkness, a single wing:
how long, soul, will the cry fall
before it is given me,
I, who will not be ready--

and the small leaves, all
that turned to face me
turn away. And now the scream--

AUTUMN EQUINOX

This is the day the salts in your hands
awake to be counted equally.
You pay out and pay out,
left, right, ebony sweats...
What torture the equipoise!
At the poles the sun, sleepless,
counts down the seconds, 3, 2, 1, , ,
And now the year steps back,
the wind, released, surrenders
to darkness the first minute--
your nerves lie down, blue and ice
frosts the ganglia, white, multifoliate.

THE MUTABILITY POEM

They might be sailors' wives,
faces set against the panes
erected by another age
but for their fingers, naked,
nubile as those of a Rubens, splayed
to raise venetian blinds,
these widows in my neighborhood.
Noon sun gathers them
one by one at ruffled portals
to watch me weed the yard
of my new house. Dew-lapped,
they flap and flubber behind glass,
arms akimbo in a sea of hips.

Now heads nod approval
counting each stem yanked up,
explosions of the roots
spraying me with dust. Lips pucker,
empurpled, to catch me stripping,
skinny-dipping my own sweat.

Ladies, I would shout out,
your lives want occupation
and your small yards fore and aft

you anchor with prepubescent boys,
would, stalk by stalk, arise
under a man's hands, little edens . . .

but we will never speak.

And in the evenings when I meander
my cool, unwieldy garden and observe
your beds so barbed they're shorn
to stand, unwavering at attention,
I stare into my roses
the former owners kept
in perfect health the realtor told me
until the husband's death,
his widow's sudden flight . . .
They are blighted, they go on blooming!
I refuse to prune them, they won't die!
The cankered, fragile, indomitable
survivals of the vanished, of the vanishers!

CROWS OVER THE WHEATFIELD

--after the painting by Vincent van Gogh

Over this landscape a face is moving.
It is not in the road turned back
at either side and at the center
writhing out of the mire
on its hind feet, unbridled.

Nor in the fields themselves.
There the wheat is a sea
reflecting nothing, raging
golden, burning eternally.

Here, at the sky, bodiless,
eyeless, scarred dark with clouds
assembling one moment its lineaments
to surrender that moment the next,
the face stares down into mine.

Out of it the silence comes
row on row, infinitesimal,
swinging, black, over the wheat
in the shape of crow
refusing to release me
until it bears me down, headfirst
into the flaming, reeling.

        Soul, oh, soul,
when I am torn from you,
will you be as nameless and as dark
as this crow, that one, that, that, that--
ascending forever, descending
over the wheat no hand will touch?

THREE SONGS FOR SOUL

I

TO THE STATUE OF A YOUNG SATYR

Soul, when you leave me
take this cast, less beautiful.

That sometime the next millennia
a boy can come to you alone.
Erect, bowlegged, smirk
flashing that grizzled thing
which bared itself to crowds
passing, incurious, centuries.

He will be beside himself.

And trembling, dumb,
hours he will stand, convulsed,
transfixed by his desire
he sees in you, such beauty.

Release him, then. That like the rest
touched by the shallows of your eye
or not, he, too, can slip away.
And he will bear such little gilt
secreted in his fist
he might consider it
chryselephantine and not himself
and less the everlasting.

II

THE LIZARD

Soul, find me an instant
when the sun swoops down
between hibiscus blossoms
posed to wash the terrace black
at their descent. Instant of sunfall
come to date palm, come to lemon
kissing lemon, instant when plum bruises pear.
Instant of bougainvillaea
the wild grape, shriveling, white.
Instant when day is a nimbus
encircling the face of a leaf.

Let it discover him, soul,
and some infinitesimal fly
remain his one companion
when his tongue flicks out and in.
Then his skin, soul, which can be dun,
jade, chartreuse, pumice at his whim,
will play out, cold a second
on sill, rock or flowerpot.
Not at the end of my life
but here---then draw it back--
Peter, breathe yourself into him.

III

SONG TO TAPIR

Soul, when I come back,
let me reside, uncomely, in this:
porcine but no pig,
equine but no horse,
a freak of nature, dappled, inviolate.
The world will visit my eyes
on the other side of moats
and the beast there will admit it:
each stare or flout, each grimace,
each finger crooked to point
will dissolve in my black depths.
Lower, this head will gnaw the grass.

What great calm we will come to
you and I, after this body,
his mind, ravening or glutted,
fall from us that last hour.

These words, too, stumbling down,
now standing, falling, I'll cast off.
And cast off, dross, and not forget
this raiment I arose to
morning after morning, this poetry.

IN WITNESS

I take the dark out of myself
and hang it on the window, calling it midnight.
I spread this oak across it, so.

I take the bird I've never seen,
whose song will break a man,
fix her to an upper branch.

Out of myself I wring the moon,
then lights which weigh my palm,
glittering like frog spawn

or eyes in a peacock's tail,
scintillant, staring back
when as stars I've hurled them out--

and now, at my desk and lamp,
in a tiny circle of calm,
all I ask for or claim,

I lift my hand, the bird starts up.
What an old song this is, a favorite,
that my voice, beside itself, rises to drown it.

THE GOLDEN RAIN TREE

After these words it will begin December
at the end of my thirty-ninth year.
Under my breath a wind will rise
to scatter birdsong, flower,
a man's long shadow on the window
violet at twilight, flickering,
drawing the night against himself.

But now there is this fall, continuous
of petal after petal on the evening,
and the sidewalk, flooded yellow
awash in mockingbird, awash in gold.

After these: blackout; a torrent on the pavement;
a man more than halfway through;
the slow, cold sentences diminishing,
refusing to diminish. After this.

IN THE CREPUSCULAR

You have but to lift your hand
and this time appears to you
between day lily, night star,
between cobalt, indigo.

You have but to give your word
to any name not your own
and through it floods such music
as becomes the sycamore,

the tree frog's obligato
skrete of cricket, the oboe
from locusts in the live oak
until this minute secret.

This is the hour of gold leaf
at the edge of your pages,
when assuming beak and claw
you take off on sudden wing,

answering cries of women
calling you to them, rising,
the honey of each moment
you imagine as you come.

You have but to lift your palm
to see how finely written,
how minute the continents
between little finger, thumb,

you to whom fire is given
for song and so intensely
you must renounce it lightly
when the darkness takes your hand.

TO A WASP CAUGHT IN THE STORM SASH AT THE ADVENT OF THE WINTER SOLSTICE

Terrorless, I awake.
This is the darkest night
the year can turn to
and I, at the middle of my life,
float up in it, twilight,
from sleep deeper than drifts
canceling rockwall, fence and hill,
all neighbors beyond the window.
Soon gifts will come,
and then good wine and talk
pour through the adjoining rooms
while fires bank and fall.
But now, inside this moment,
between the cerulean panes,
your wizened, tiny, moronic
St. Vitus' wiggle
draws the night sky down around it.
What brings your rasping to this edge
between one blue world and the next?
My face warping the glass?
My soul against your song?

THE LAST TESTAMENT OF PIERRE DUVAL

THE LAST TESTAMENT OF PIERRE DUVA

From the air the island is a skull,
a dog's head mounted on a pike,
a snake engorged.
At the mouths are white sand beaches
where I might lie down,
rinsed in light, burying myself.

Men learn how to die here.
It is this sea that teaches them,
mute, indivisible, emptying their faces,
demanding nothing but the absolute
and their bodies, blue and cold, rising.

Scarlet, the jungle spreads my lap,
heart-shaped at the interior.
Trees crosshatch
the dead center tourists never enter.

***

The baths are closed,
the waters black pits from my window.
My pilot cannot move
his tongue without stammering.
I ask why each few inches
dolphins lap the breakers on my map.
Always-until-we-die, he points,
they-are-with-us, look below.
Frozen, I see water, I see nothing.

As we descend, bathhouses arise
under his hands, endless
rooftops like headstones
shimmering at noon. I am so numb
I should be perched among them,

a seagull staring out to sea.

58

***

My pensione is unknown, still
but for the German, a few Italians.
I sleep till noon, I eat alone
among servants who keep their color
pushing my table to the sea.
Their talk swarms like gnats,
a shower of mosquitoes. I am better.
My chills are burning off.
And when I reach out, I can touch my body.

***

I have heard the tiger.
He guards the colony
in the jungle where incurables
lie generations with their own.
My houseboy tells me he is cu-r-ed
and, like the others exiled
from the interior, stammers.
He swears their elders speak
only in rhyme and at the center
their song is too pure for human ears.
Under the tiger's cry I stretch
cool, reddening with fever.

***

The young no longer come here,
only the survivors, lap robes propped
along stone benches of the esplanade.
In the cemetery of the rich
there are no longer enough bodies.
My legs, rippling, stiffen,
wading the tombs and chickweed,
the fallen angel, hacked up marble.

***

The dictator walked out,

lacking survivors, into the waves.
I have seen his spirit hovering
the pink marble wharves,
a dragonfly before the rain.

His garden flames, the weeds
violet on the statues, cerulean.
He bought "The Dying Gaul,"
"The Discus Thrower," others.
They will outlast the trees.

***

Through stained glass windows
last light dances on the palace floor
chasing the squirrels, lavender on marble.
I stand in the abandoned foyer.
On the landing a woman's face
smiles, now is swallowed by the shadow.
My body is a black vase.
My body is a white vase.
I carry it through these rooms.
I would pour myself out here, ashes.

***

The yellow dog that follows me,
the yellow shadow,
the mouth that never closes
and out of which the hours come
stiff in a procession,
the streets baring their wounds--
the yellow streets he takes me down,
cul-de-sacs where I am hiding,
numinous, my sweat gleaming,
my cry one word--
for this I have come here.
The day rises, the day dies
in the jaws of the dog
where I burn off, I am burning.

                    ***

The glacéed, the sautéed, the black butters--
I am a work of art
with each course I command
then refuse to eat, seated among flies
performing my service on the terrace.
Before the waiter clears, a draught,
a crust, I will let cross my lips.
I will leave the sacrifice on fire.

                    ***

Their toll has rung me
to the cathedral square
shunned by the natives.
Under these bells the beggars hang
on rags and sticks, a stench
like the drains' black water.
One holds a cup between his teeth.
I empty my wallet, my pockets, into it.
I would give everything
to lie like him, armless,
blind, legless, under the clappers.

                    ***

I would be this wheel
never ceasing, the die cast
and cast again, the green oasis
at the gaming table.
In the croupier's smile
I lose myself each night
watching the bones dance.
I am the bliss, delirious, of loss.

                    ***

The terror of a clear sky.
The sea, too, clear, unmoving.
Under their eyes I have stretched out

bronzing like the statues.

And then the scream, the gulls
carrying the rain behind them.
I am cast under its hands
enduring, almost perfect.

Now when the blood comes
I am blood, the cough ecstatic.

***

The German tells me
the sea will come to us
speaking in tongues, three-legged
at the end of time. I am not certain.
I knew the sea's face
this morning a few moments
when the native drew that monster
still quivering from the deep.
And while it died,
its stare stood, cold, in my blood.

Tonight the natives mourn
the death of another god.
The land wind killed it.
I will not die under these eyes.

***

I will have my last woman,
the widow of the dictator.

A pauper, she comes for a song.
My houseboy arranges this
if I will pay him with my robe,
the black moiré she peels off quickly.

She has come and gone.
Twice over, I was only bone

drowning to weigh anchor.
We never spoke, her skin
fell like peau de soie about her.

                    ***

Last night the dolphin came
at my first call, a shadow
under the full moon, silver
taking my breath.

I waited the whole night,
a body only on this beach.
At first light his fin surfaced.
Now I know whorls inside a shell,
secrets men wait for
stopping their eyes and ears
with emerald going down.

In that silence of the sea's floor
I have rested. The sea ends.
I will not die by water.
I have been there.

                    ***

In the interior there are trees
from the Stone Age,
my houseboy tells me, forests
where the sun is seen at noon
midsummer if at all.
Here spiders swim the trees
giant as cats and you are borne
back to their beds, venturing too close.
Here the incurables lie down
tangling their limbs to make a child.
Here they take the dark
into their mouths finally.

                    ***

The point of rocks is orange
at sunset, the sea orange
rising to strike it. Now the grotto
I stoop to enter. How cold the light
around the sibyl's face, her single wish
she chants, fingering grains of sand.
And when I near her, I am warm
knowing her wish mine. And when I leave
my release is almost final.

       ***

Swear to me I will not return,
I beg my houseboy I have bribed
to leave me at the jungle's edge.
He will swear nothing.
He tells me I may come back
a-sal-a-man-der-like-this, Master.
And he extends a lizard on his palm,
the green sac twitching at its throat
bulbous. Everything I carried here
I have offered him to give this up.
It remains my sole vexation.

       ***

He calls himself a doctor.
But he trims my hair and beard,
applies balm only to my face,
he makes me to lie down in camphor.
He sells me perfumes to take with me,
unguents, frankincense.

Under his razor I am cooling,
a new man, and on his window
I think I see the jungle blazing
scarlet at sunset.
Here a naked breast, an arm,
golden, the eyes, the privates
all severed, all perfected.

64

***

I have told the gull this morning
tomorrow I will be emptied of you.
Tomorrow of you, I tell the statues
strolling among them, laving my body
deep purple with the salves.

And tonight I am wrapped in light,
chanting to myself, sitting out
on the esplanade, this stone bench
holding my terror, telling myself
I may return, the lees precious
no longer in my glass.

And tomorrow when stars appear
over the island, this bench will wait.
And the dark will settle on it,
and Absence stretch his legs and Night
will take my name a second
while they sever me to her lips
and then, sated, turn away.

And if I cross the tiger's path
while he sleeps, I will kneel
with spiders who know my prayer
and my throat will swell, one cry
deeper than the sea could answer.

I will no longer be this head,
this maw, aching, this sex
where the years have come to drink
like vermin to the river.

And then the elders will receive me,
my soul my body
dancing before them naked.
And the darkness will burn off

as they scatter me and the pain
hacked up and will burn off and burn off.

And then the cry which will be with me
when I am no one will lie down
beside me and my absence
will rise, answering it forever.

SUCH COMFORT AS THE NIGHT

THE NIGHT SPEAKS TO A MAN

To begin with, she promises nothing.
She tells him how far she has journeyed
merely to say this: how mountains
fell under her step and surrendered
the snow of their shadows in passing;
how rivers stood back and then parted
their waters' still centers, empurpled.
How the nightbirds rode the underside
of her great wings, how trees gave up their roots.
Then the wind shifts and she pledges
she will stretch out now beneath him
and, stammering, he may enter
and take down her sky--
this sky at the back of their breath--
illimitable, before all language.

SUCH COMFORT AS THE NIGHT CAN BRING TO US

A man and a woman walk out into the summer night.
All evening they have been fighting
and now, arms intertwined, their bodies
wrung with sweat, they ache
numb, to be speechless,
delivered of each other.

Let the night speak then.
First to the woman that she turn to him
here, by the river lifting already to them
the face of its black depths. Then to the man
that he draw her down beneath the willows
where they trade shadows, trade them back
as in the falling light they bartered words,
swapping the coinage weightless.

Let the night sing then.
Let it ring dumb the chorus
of that other life, echoless
in root and vein, rock sucking at the wave
or in midair a note struck warbling.

As in that other time the night played, mute,
walking the garden noons--
where it strolled later in the cool--
before men, before women,
language, their shadows known to them
in parting only, and all flesh ravaging.

SONNET

To love a woman
is to go down to the sea again.
I said: to love the same woman
is to pitch a tent beside the tides
no matter how they read.
And then to ride them, moiling,
season unto season.
                  I say:
surrendering, to be taken in
as if assuming illimitable waters.
That all things now are possible
you pretend time and time again
coming together. All things solid ground
in such breakers as you walk on after.

NIGHTPIECE

Nightwind on the jasmine, rattling its censer,
the air opaque with little wings, risen scents.
Leaning together, nightpalms sway,
a chorus, nightbirds in unison.

A nightshape spiders the terrace,
finds its counterpart, seizes, stings.
And behind drawn shades a manshape,
nightshaped for you, lady,
laid out in the nightdark,
extends it to you. And all night gives way.

NECESSITIES

Between a man and a woman
lying down together, rising
together, over the years
a profusion of silence will blossom.

Upside down in the dirt
its taproot lashed to the wind
from which it sucks until giddy, frizzled,
their plant will cast petals on bedrock.

And what words these are,
all unspoken! Scabrous and twitchy,
the blooms blue-veined and nacreous,
intertwined. Out of such coupling
invisible to all but them
the hill is sewn with burdock
against the torrents of the rain
and fields run wild, burgeoning,
up to the edges of each separate house
lit tonight against the dark
where a man, a woman
shut themselves in.

AFTER MEN, AFTER WOMEN

Because I long to be some other
and my body is too much Peter
to release a man, I turn to you.
Sometimes you disappoint me.
Satisfied to be a woman
you have no need of the blind sea
or shore, steeped in radiance,
where we crawled up and for that second
last night traded faces
and all parts, traded wings
and all breath, numinous and passing.

THE GULL

After the more than momentary calm
which lifted me, when I arose
out of your body, I was no one.

I was not a man, nor was I woman
I had become that last second
swimming across your breath.

Nor was my voice the silence
which pooled about us as the aftermath
drew back the tide and left us, gasping.

I was this white wing, acetylene.
And while I burned on the horizon,
the gulf wind bearing me along
and surrendered, dazed, to sleep,
I was this calling in each pinion
for nothing, its chill reaches
I was this shrill, unending scream.

And sleep spread you for the night air--
I was this flame, beating on itself--
the thick, black current of the world,
which took you, undiminished, vanquishing.

THE CARP POND

But for such flashes between the lilies
of what is vanishing, their flames fan-tailed,
this sky might fall here eternally,
the features of midday its face,
the features of absence its night.

Only their chill fire will push it back.

We whose voice swells the pond
we cannot rise to like the carp,
their gold snouts' bubbles floating up
across the water we will never cross,
we who return your stare
only slack-jawed in grief or beached
granite-eyed or no one
swimming in ourselves,
Heaven, remember us.

CHRYSANTHEMUM LIGHT

The last afternoon of your life
ask them that you be taken out
into this garden. Let the night descend,
plum-swollen and plum-sweet,
bruised with its own juices
and dark perfume. Let it be still
where the moonlight beads
at the fern's underleaf,
the espalier jasmine clambers,
the peach trees, bloated, overripe.

Later, you will recall
only the small cusps of flame
the chrysanthemums extended
as the night bared its wounds
in pith or resin; the white blood
at camellia's lips, agape;
willows the thunder cleaves; the lilies
hurling down trumpets, their shorn bud.

And the stump uprooting itself to walk,
this you will recall. And the afterlight
which draws you down upon it
until you have such body
as night itself, walking the garden
in the cool of your voice.

While the plums will rain, the peaches,
over these beds in flame
and this small soul
you carried here will drop and fall away.

And black fire call to black,
white fire to white, and in your face
the garden will lie down,
rise and surrender
as if it might be everlasting.

LINES FOR A SLEEPING CHILD

When you came forward,
bearing your mother's body
into such season as the rain describes
with black ice, that spring the face of granite,
I took you, stillborn, for a monster.

Now, a year later, I have settled
into your death. And I continue it,
bending this moment above your older sister
who floats out on the great swells of her first sleep.

Numinous, ruddy in the moonlight,
her little forehead kisses sharp as apples,
kisses as sweet. We both know
you would have liked to taste like that.

Here, on trees that gnarl skyward
sometimes the blossoms will catch fire
and from them burst such roundness, fecund.

I would have taught you
how high you have to climb for them.

TOWARD MORNING

In the absence of others
I make do with the sky,

Gemini, Taurus
and Scorpio, my own,

this same sky I've carried
on my head like a tribesman

balancing a basket of knives
my whole life.

I make do with the first light,
the street violet,

washed in quiet
as after the thunder pauses

when no one dares come out.
I am alive in this moment

shredding a single leaf
I carried all night

like a talisman I charmed
only to work in the dark--

and the next moment and the next--
with no name for tomorrow,

the brother I never lived up to,
or the past, that cousin

too many times removed.
Sometimes, at moments like these,

I almost believe again
in a god who reveals himself

through the bole of an oak
or the moon, scattering its branches

on this sidewalk, lifting a step
upwards, a second

disappearing my next step.

THE OTHER

When you come to the other side
of lust the body lays itself
down in others as itself
no longer and the fields till now
fallow, bloom, vermillion.

When you cross to the other side
of pride the heart withers
into tinder, the wind blesses it.
Your body flares, white sticks
this side of anger.

Arriving at the other side
of terror the voice is a dark flame
walking evenings in the garden,
your name unknown to it
if the last light calls you.

And when you have passed the other side
of hope the shore will blaze
finally. We are all light here.
Do not look for me or ask.
You will never have known me.